Rayan

my Book

Grade 1

Modules 3-4

Authors and Advisors

Alma Flor Ada • Kylene Beers • F. Isabel Campoy

Joyce Armstrong Carroll • Nathan Clemens

Anne Cunningham • Martha C. Hougen • Tyrone C. Howard

Elena Izquierdo • Carol Jago • Erik Palmer

Robert E. Probst • Shane Templeton • Julie Washington

Contributing Consultants

David Dockterman • Jill Eggleton

Printed in the U.S.A.

ISBN   978-0-358-46145-6

10   0868   29 28 27 26 25 24 23

4500867685

r1.21

MODULE 3

Amazing Animals

MODULE 4

Better Together

🌐 **SOCIAL STUDIES CONNECTION:**

OPINION WRITING

by Jane Medina • illustrated by Maine Diaz
INFORMATIONAL TEXT

by Rozanne Lanczak Williams
INFORMATIONAL TEXT

tap-tap-tap

my house

Amazing Animals

"Little by little the bird makes his nest."

—American Proverb

How do animals' bodies help them?

knock-
knock

Get Curious
Video

Words About How Animals Live

Complete the Vocabulary Network to show what you know about the words.

camouflage

Meaning: Camouflage is what hides something or makes it difficult to see.

Synonyms and Antonyms	Drawing

mammal

Meaning: A **mammal** is a kind of animal that has hair and feeds milk to its babies.

Synonyms and Antonyms	Drawing

characteristics

Meaning: **Characteristics** are things that make a person, animal, or thing different from others.

Synonyms and Antonyms	Drawing

Animal Q & A

Imagine that *you* had wings! What could *you* do? Find out what animals can do with *their* bodies!

Zip, zip, zip!

Knock, knock!

Q: What could you do with **wings?**

A: **Swim!** Penguins flap to go fast!

Q: What could you do with a **shell?**

A: **Hide!** Turtles are safe inside.

Whoosh!

Zzzzzzzz...

Q: What could you do
with a **trunk?**

A: Snorkel! Elephants
get air like this.

Q: What could you do
with **claws?**

A: Grab! Bats hang upside
down to sleep.

Prepare to Read

GENRE STUDY **Realistic fiction** stories are made up but could happen in real life. Look for:

- characters and a setting that seem real
- ways the pictures and words work together to tell the story

SET A PURPOSE **Ask questions** before, during, and after you read to help you understand the text. Look for evidence in the text and pictures to **answer** your questions.

POWER WORDS

exclaimed

twigs

surprise

soon

warm

empty

Meet Nina de Polonia.

The Nest

by Carole Roberts

illustrated by Nina de Polonia

"Max! Jen!" exclaimed Quin. "Look! I see a nest!"

The nest was made of twigs.

It had grass in it.

"The grass will make it soft," said Ben.

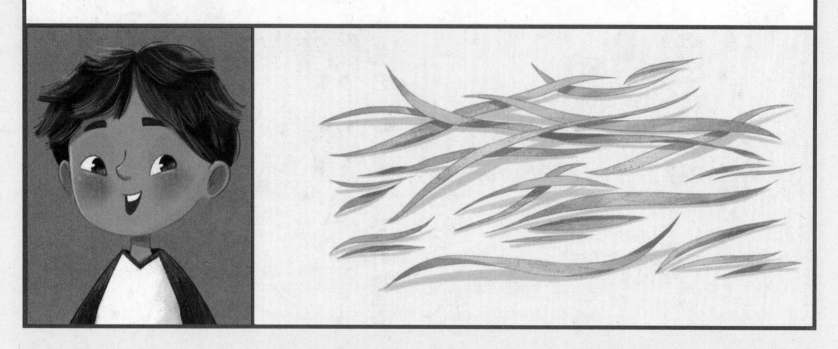

"I see twigs and leaves," said Wes.

"I see bits of paper," said Liz.

"We can write about it!" said Jen.

One day, a surprise
was in the nest.

"Eggs!" the kids said.
"We see eggs with dots!"

"We will look at the nest every day," said Mrs. Web.

"Will we see baby birds?" asked Quin.
"Soon?" everyone asked.

The bird sat on the nest.
This made the eggs warm.

The bird sat and sat for days.

One day, the kids see baby birds!

The mom fed the baby birds.

The dad fed the baby birds.

"The baby birds look soft," said Liz.

"Soon they will get big feathers," said Quin.

Every day, the birds try to fly.

"Can they fly yet?" the kids asked.

22

The baby birds try.

Then the baby birds can fly!

One day, it was quiet.

The nest was empty.

It was fun to see the baby birds!

Turn and Talk

Use details from **The Nest** to answer these questions with a partner.

1. **Ask and Answer Questions** What questions did you ask yourself before, during, and after reading? How did they help you understand **The Nest**?

2. What important things happen after the bird lays the eggs?

Talking Tip

Be polite. Wait for your turn to tell your idea to your partner.

I think that _____.

Write a Journal Entry

PROMPT Think about what the birds did in **The Nest.** Write a journal entry to show what you learned.

PLAN First, draw a picture that shows an interesting fact you learned about birds or eggs.

WRITE Now write today's date. Write a sentence or two to explain the information your picture shows. Remember to:

- Begin the name of the month with a capital letter.

- Be sure each sentence tells a complete idea.

I learned baby birds can fly.

Prepare to Read

GENRE STUDY **Folktales** are stories from long ago that have been told over and over. Look for:

- animals that act and talk like people
- storytelling phrases like **long ago**
- the reason an author tells a story

SET A PURPOSE Make pictures in your mind as you read. Words that tell how things look, sound, feel, taste, or smell and words about feelings can help you **create mental images**.

POWER WORDS
dull
thank
once

Meet James Bruchac.

Blue Bird and Coyote

a Native American tale, as told by James Bruchac

illustrated by Chris Lensch

Long ago, Blue Bird was not blue.
She was gray and dull.
How did she get her color?

One day, Gray Bird saw a lake.

It was beautiful!

A blue butterfly was at the lake.

"How did you get your color?"
asked Gray Bird.
"It is from the lake," said Butterfly.

"This is how to get it," said Butterfly.
"Go in the lake.
Do it four days in a row.
Then thank the lake."

Day 1

Day 2

Day 3

Day 4

Gray Bird did this.
Then she was blue!
"Thank you, lake!"

Long ago, Coyote was green.

Coyote saw Blue Bird.

"How did you get your color?" asked Coyote.

"I will tell you," said Blue Bird.

And she did.

Coyote went in the lake.
But, he did all four dips in one day!
Once he was blue, Coyote got out.
He did not thank the lake.

Coyote ran off to tell his friends.
But Coyote fell!
He went down,
down,
down a big hill.

Coyote got up.
Now he was all dusty and dull!

To this day, Blue Bird is blue.
And Coyote is dusty gray.

READ
Together

Use details from **Blue Bird and Coyote** to answer these questions with a partner.

1. **Create Mental Images** What pictures did you make in your mind when Blue Bird and Coyote got their colors? What words helped you create those pictures?

2. What do you think the author wants you to learn from the story?

Listening Tip

Listen carefully. Think about the meaning of what your partner is saying.

Write a Story Ending

PROMPT Coyote still wants blue fur! How will he get it? Make up an ending to add to **Blue Bird and Coyote**.

PLAN What is Coyote's new plan to get blue fur? Add three ideas to the chart.

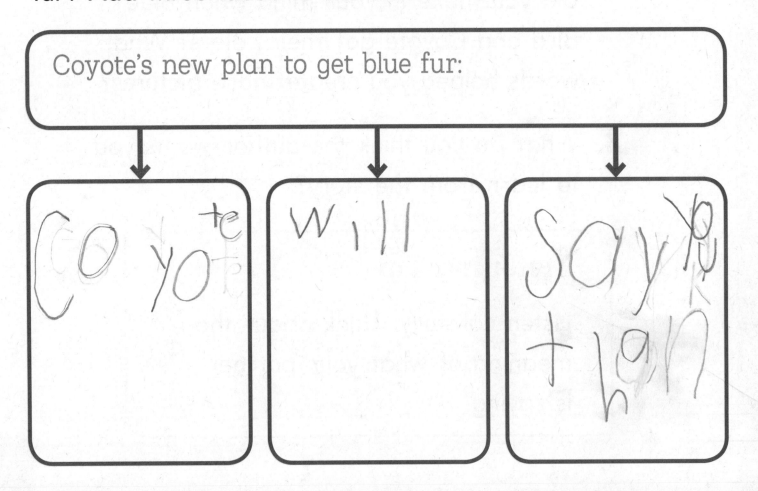

Coyote's new plan to get blue fur:

Coyote	will	say to t han

WRITE Now write what happens next in the story. Use another sheet of paper if you need to. Remember to:

- Tell how Coyote solves his problem.

- Be sure each sentence tells a complete idea.

Prepare to Read

GENRE STUDY **Narrative nonfiction** gives information but sounds like a story. Look for:

- information about something real
- words that describe sounds and things
- a real setting

SET A PURPOSE As you read, stop and think if you don't understand something. Reread, look at the pictures, use what you already know, or ask yourself questions to help you figure it out.

Meet Kenard Pak.

HAVE YOU HEARD THE NESTING BIRD?

by Rita Gray   illustrated by Kenard Pak

44

Mourning doves take their morning stroll.

coah, cooo, cooo, coooo

Woodpecker calls from
a tree with a hole.

cuk-cuk-cuk-cuk-cuk

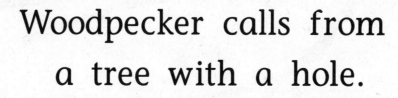

Starling sings from a metal pole.

whistle-ee-wee-tree

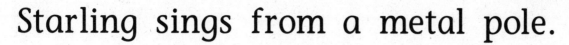

But have you heard the nesting bird?
"What bird? Where?"
"That robin, nesting up there."

Sparrow makes a simple jingle.

chiddik, chiddik

Swallow slides from under a shingle.

ha-ha-chit-chit-chit,
ha-ha-twitter-twit!

Crow calls out,
"Come meet and mingle!"
caw! caw! caw! caw!

But have you heard the nesting bird?
"Not a single tweet or trill."
"This nesting bird is so still!"

Cardinal wears a pointy hat.
*cheer-cheer-cheer-
purdy-purdy-purdy*

Chickadee is an acrobat.
chick-a-dee-dee-dee

Catbird sounds like a hungry cat.
meow! meow!

But have you heard
the nesting bird?
"It doesn't sing, not even a bit!"
"All it does is sit and sit."

Blue jay's shriek is
as sharp as a drill.

jay! jay!   jay! jay!

Whip-poor-will has
his favorite trill.

whip-poor-will   whip-poor-will

Wood thrush turns
the twilight still.

ee-oh-lay   ee-oh-laaay

But have you heard the nesting bird?
"It hasn't sung a single song."
"This bird has been sitting for so long!"

Wait, what's that . . . ?

Tapping   Cracking

"Something made a little sound!"

Breaking   Shaking

"The bird is starting to move around!"

Ruffling   Shuffling

"The bird flew off with something blue."

Cheeping   Peeping

"Look! Another robin is coming too!"

"The baby birds are here!"

HAVE YOU HEARD THE NESTING BIRD?

by Rita Gray illustrated by Kenard Pak

Turn and Talk

Use details from **Have You Heard the Nesting Bird?** to answer these questions with a partner.

1. **Monitor and Clarify** When you came to a part of the text you did not understand, what did you do to try to figure it out?

2. Why does the nesting bird sit so long?

Talking Tip

Ask a question if you are not sure about your partner's ideas.

Why did you say _____?

Write a Story

PROMPT Imagine that you are with the kids
in **Have You Heard the Nesting Bird?**
What do you see the nesting bird do?

PLAN Draw pictures to show the main things
the nesting bird does **first**, **next**, and **last**.

First	Next	Last
First the bird makes a nest.	Next the bird keep eggs warm.	Last the baby birds are here.

WRITE Now write your own version of the story. Tell what you saw the nesting bird do. Use another sheet of paper if you need it. Remember to:

- Use **first, next,** and **last** to show the order of events.

- Use words to describe the nesting bird.

first next last

63

Prepare to Read

GENRE STUDY **Procedural texts** tell how to do or make something. Look for:

- directions to follow
- numbered steps that are in order
- pictures that help you understand

SET A PURPOSE Use the topic of the text and important details to help you **summarize.** Use your own words to retell.

Meet Steve Jenkins
and Robin Page.

Step-by-Step Advice

from the

Animal Kingdom

by Steve Jenkins & Robin Page

from **How to Swallow a Pig**

How to
Defend
Yourself
Like an Armadillo

1 Freeze!

Many predators don't notice prey unless it's moving. Holding still can be a good tactic.

2 Run.

Armadillos can move quickly. So can you. If freezing doesn't work, don't just sit there.

3 Dig.

Start digging a hole. Use your long claws. Work quickly! You'll soon have a burrow to hide in.

4 Swim.

You're a good swimmer. And not
every predator likes to get wet.

5 Leap.

Try jumping a few feet up into the air.
This can startle even the fiercest predator.
It can give you time to escape.

6 Hunker down.

If all else fails, pull in your head
and feet. And hope your armor
persuades the attacker to give up.

How to
Spin a Web
Like a Spider

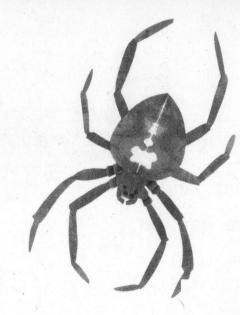

① Cast a line.

Cast a single silk thread into the air. If you're lucky, the breeze will catch it. It will snag on a nearby branch or other object.

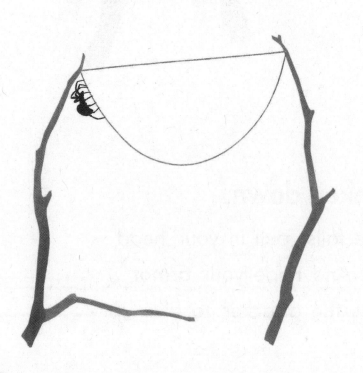

② Make a loop.

Walk across the first thread. Spin another that droops to form a U.

3 Turn your U into a Y.

Drop a line from the bottom of the loose thread. Tighten it to make a Y shape.

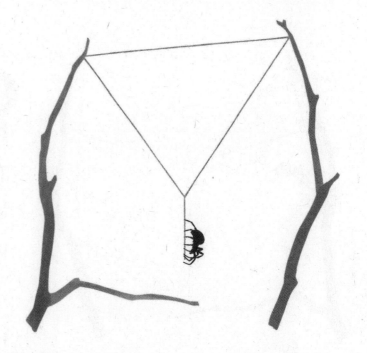

4 Frame your web.

Spin threads that will form the borders of your web.

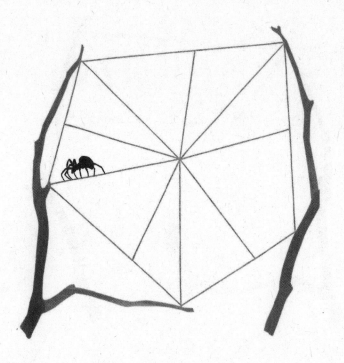

⑤ Spin threads from the center to the edges.

These lines form the framework for your web. They give you unsticky threads to walk on.

⑥ Make a spiral.

Make a spiral of silk. So far, none of the threads you've spun are sticky.

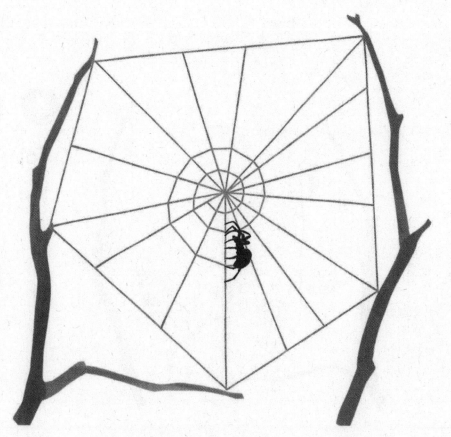

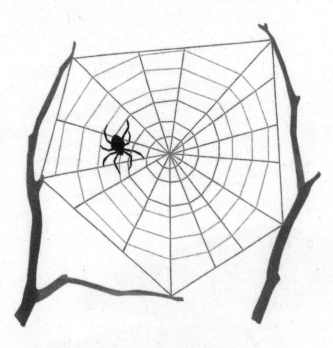

⑦ Get sticky.

Now work your way back to the center.
Lay down sticky threads. The original
spiral will be your path. You'll recycle
it by eating it as you go.

⑧ Wait for dinner.

Now you can rest. Sit in
the center of your new web.
Wait for an insect to blunder
into your trap.

How to
Trap Fish
Like a Humpback Whale

1 **Find some fish.**

The first step is locating a school of fish. Some of these schools include millions of fish.

2 **Tell your friends.**

Call any humpbacks in the area. Let them know you've located dinner.

③ Slap the surface.

Whacking the water with your tail frightens the fish. It makes them swim closer together. If you don't have a tail, ask one of the whales for help.

④ Swim in circles.

Join the whales in circling beneath the fish. Blow bubbles. Herd the fish together by swimming in smaller and smaller circles.

5 Gulp!

Take turns swimming up.
Open your mouth wide.
Swallow as many fish as
you can in one gulp.

Turn and Talk

Use details from **Step-by-Step Advice from the Animal Kingdom** to answer these questions with a partner.

1. Summarize What are the most important ideas this text is about?

2. Which animal's body helps it the best? Use ideas from the text to tell why.

Talking Tip

Wait for your turn to talk. Explain your ideas and feelings clearly.

I feel that _____.

Write a Fact

PROMPT You learned a lot about animals in **Step-by-Step Advice from the Animal Kingdom**. What was the most interesting fact?

PLAN First, draw a picture of the animal and write words to tell about the most interesting fact.

WRITE Now write your fact. Use your picture and notes for ideas. Remember to:

- Tell true information.

- Be sure your sentence tells a complete idea.

Prepare to View

GENRE STUDY **Videos** are short movies. Some videos give information. Others are for you to watch for enjoyment. Watch and listen for:

- information about the topic
- how the pictures and words work together

SET A PURPOSE Find out about beavers! Notice what the beavers do and how the events are shown in the order that they happen during the year. Think about how having the events in order helps you understand the video.

Build Background: Beaver Dams

Beaver Family

from National Geographic Kids

As You View Notice how the video has a beginning, middle, and end. The events happen in order. How does this help you understand the video? Use the words and pictures to find out what the beavers do before, during, and after winter.

Beaver
Family
from National Geographic Kids

Use details from **Beaver Family** to answer these questions with a partner.

1. **Chronological Order** What important things do beavers do before winter? What do they do during winter? Then what do they do in the spring?

2. How does a beaver use its body to build a dam?

Listening Tip

Listen carefully. Make connections. How is what your partner says like other things you know?

Let's Wrap Up!

(?) **Essential Question**

How do animals' bodies help them?

Pick one of these activities to show what you have learned about the topic.

1. **Animal <u>Do</u>s and <u>Don't</u>s**

Pick an animal you have read about. Talk to a partner. Describe what the animal should do and should not do to survive. Complete these sentences:

Do _____.

Don't _____.

2. Animal Babies

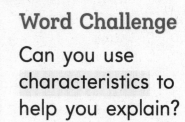

Draw a picture of one of the animals you read about. Write to explain how the mom or dad animal would take care of the babies. Share your writing with classmates.

Word Challenge

Can you use characteristics to help you explain?

My Notes

Better Together

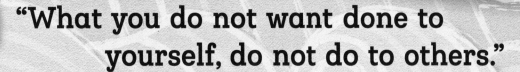

"What you do not want done to yourself, do not do to others."

—Confucius

Why is it important to do my best and get along with others?

Get Curious Video

85

Words About Being Good Citizens

Complete the Vocabulary Network to show what you
know about the words.

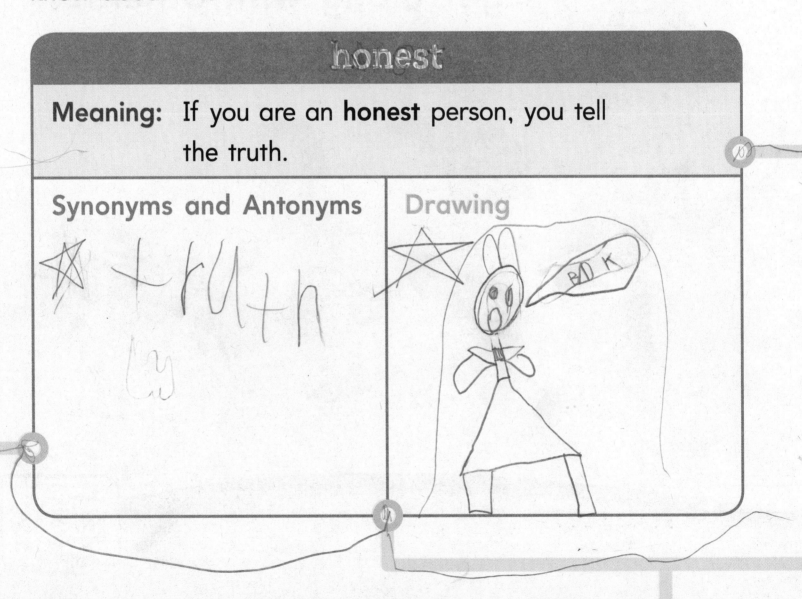

honest

Meaning: If you are an **honest** person, you tell
the truth.

Synonyms and Antonyms

truth
ly

Drawing

BOK

sport

Meaning: A good **sport** plays fair and gets along with others.

Synonyms and Antonyms	Drawing
 good game	

courtesy

Meaning: If you do something as a **courtesy**, you do it to be kind or polite.

Synonyms and Antonyms	Drawing
 good person	

GOOD SPORTS

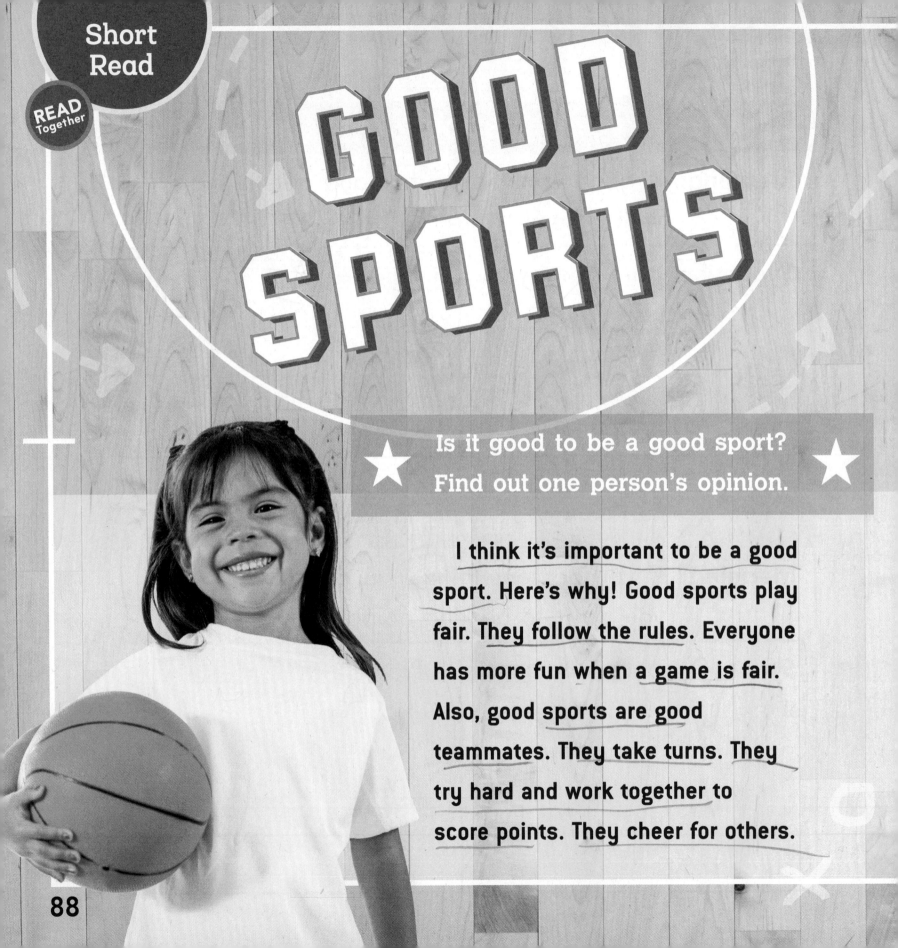

★ Is it good to be a good sport? Find out one person's opinion. ★

I think it's important to be a good sport. Here's why! Good sports play fair. They follow the rules. Everyone has more fun when a game is fair. Also, good sports are good teammates. They take turns. They try hard and work together to score points. They cheer for others.

We did it!

Your turn!

Finally, good sports are nice to be with. They don't get grouchy about who wins or loses. They think it's fun just to play! So, be a good sport. You will have fun, and others will, too!

Prepare to Read

GENRE STUDY **Informational text** is nonfiction. It gives facts about a topic or real people. Look for:

- photographs of a real person
- facts about real events
- pictures with labels

POWER WORDS

team
equipment
coach
rules
goal
fan

SET A PURPOSE Think about the author's words as you read. Then decide, or **evaluate**, which details are the most important to help you understand the text.

Meet Jane Medina.

GOAL!

by Jane Medina

illustrated by Maine Diaz

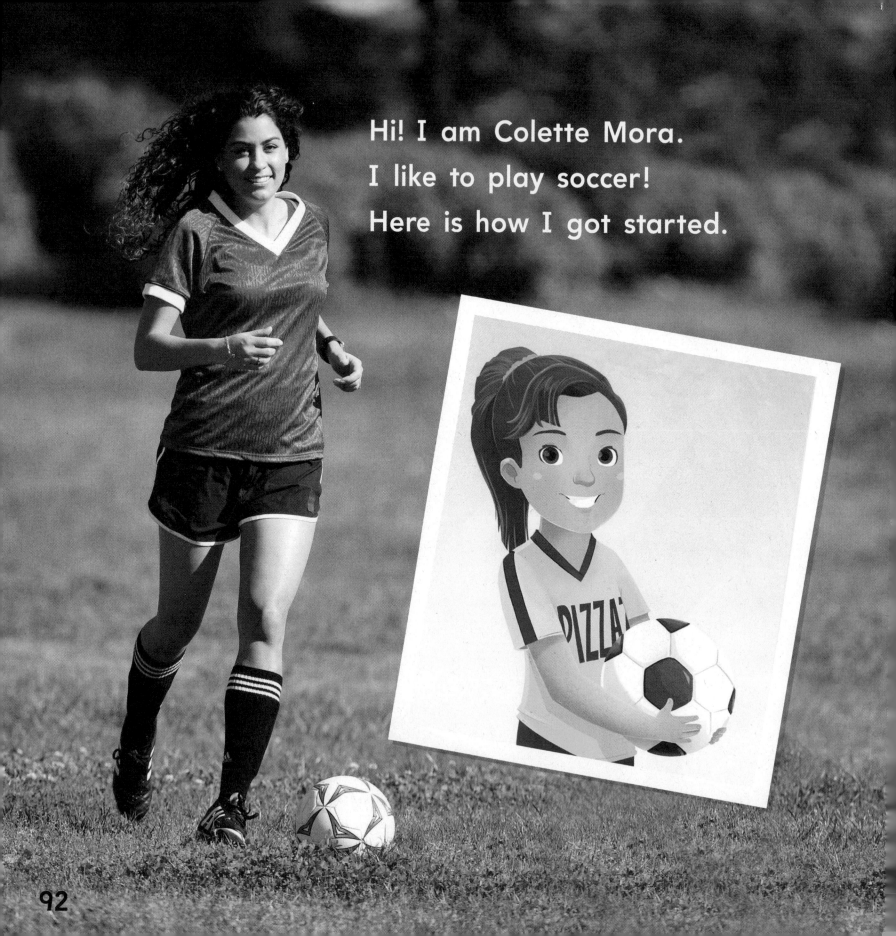

Hi! I am Colette Mora.
I like to play soccer!
Here is how I got started.

Today I get to be on my very first soccer team!
I see my twin Yvonne and my friend Brittney.

smile

ball

sock

cleats

shin guard

We have our equipment.
We will have such fun!

Mr. Chan will coach us.

"Pick a number for your uniform," he tells us.

Yvonne picks six.

Brittney picks ten.

I pick 12.

I am at my first practice.
Coach tells us the rules.
"Kick the ball.
Do not use your hands.
But the goalie *can* use her
hands to get the ball."

96

"The rules help you play fair and be safe.
Then we can *all* have fun!"

Coach tells us how to pass the ball.

I kick it, and Brittney kicks it back.

Coach tells us how to dribble the ball.

"Kick it a little.

Then run to it," he tells us.

Kick, run, kick, run, kick, run.
Little by little, we find out how
to play soccer.

I am at my first game.
The referee tells us to play fair.
Then we play!

I pass the ball to Brittney.

She kicks it to Yvonne.

Kick, pass, kick, pass.

Yvonne kicks it back to me.

I dribble the ball.

"Run, Colette!" Coach yells.

I am very quick!

The goalie runs to get the ball.

I kick it at the net. Then . . .

GOAL!

I got my very first goal!

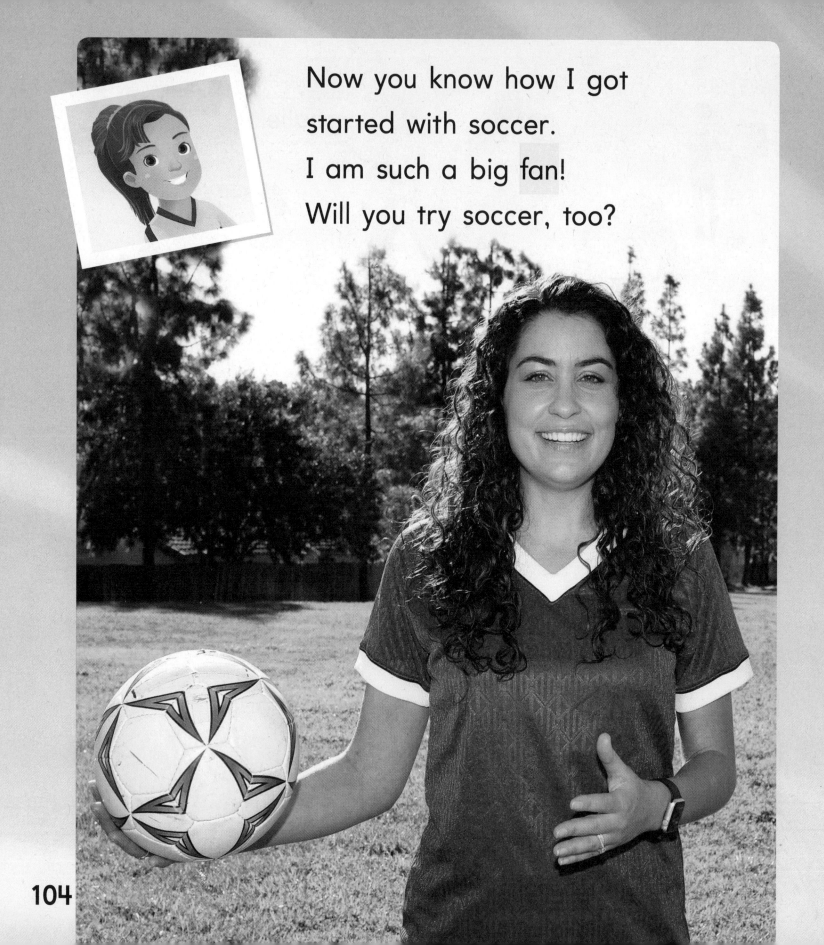

Now you know how I got started with soccer.
I am such a big fan!
Will you try soccer, too?

Turn and Talk

Use details from **Goal!** to answer these questions with a partner.

1. **Evaluate** Which details in **Goal!** are the most important for helping you understand why Colette likes soccer?

2. How do Colette and her team feel when she gets a goal? Why?

Talking Tip

Wait for your turn to talk. Explain your ideas and feelings clearly.

I think that _____.

Write Game Rules

PROMPT How do you play soccer? Use details from the words and pictures in **Goal!** to explain the rules you learned.

PLAN First, write important words from **Goal!** that tell about playing soccer.

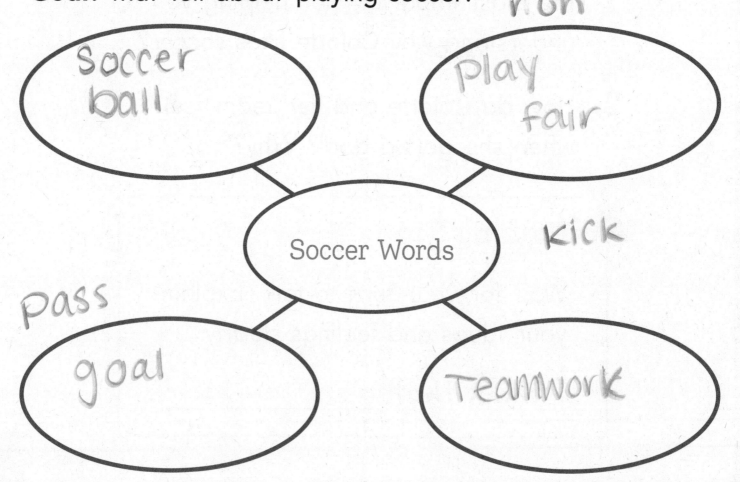

cleats

run

Soccer ball

Play fair

kick

Soccer Words

Pass

goal

Teamwork

WRITE Now write the rules for playing soccer in your own words. Remember to:

- Use soccer words from your web.

- Use verbs to tell about actions.

kick the ball

PLAY fair

Prepare to Read

GENRE STUDY **Informational text** is nonfiction. It gives facts about a topic. Look for:

- headings that stand out
- photographs
- a chart that shows information

POWER WORDS

well
exercise
body

SET A PURPOSE Read to find out the most important ideas in each part. Then **synthesize**, or put the ideas together in your mind, to find out new things about the text and what it really means to you.

Meet Rozanne Lanczak Williams.

Get UP and GO!

by Rozanne Lanczak Williams

Why Exercise?

When you are healthy, you are well.

You can get healthy and fit.

How? Exercise!

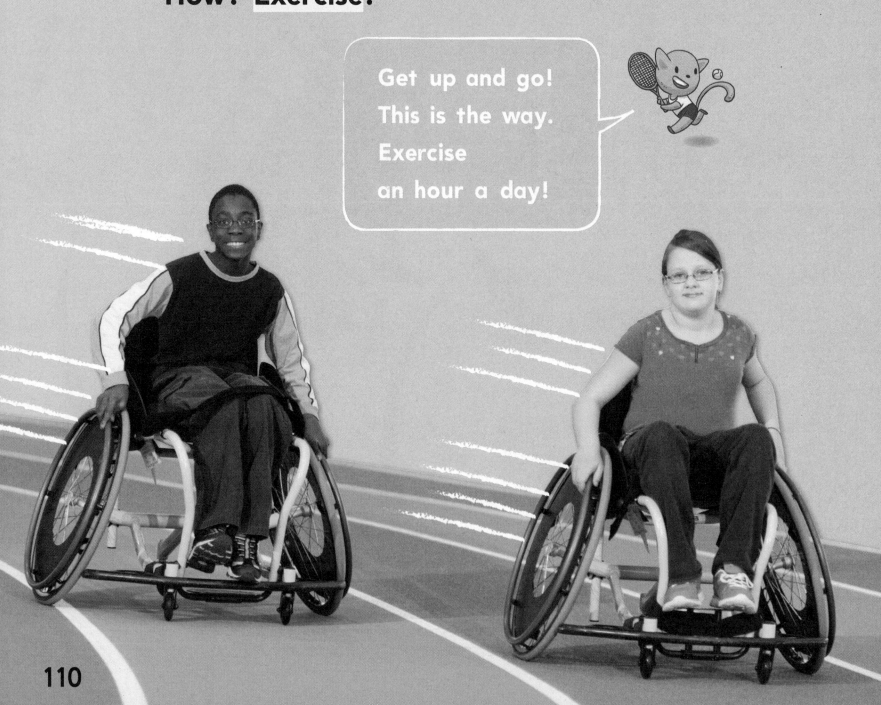

Get up and go!
This is the way.
Exercise
an hour a day!

Exercise Every Day

How can you get exercise?
You could walk.
Walk as much as you can!

A walk is great!
It is fun to skate!

Exercise with Friends

You could swim and hike with friends.
Many kids like bikes.

Play a Game

You could play hopscotch.
You could play fetch with your dog.

Jump and hop.
Play games with Pop.

Get Set . . .

It is good to stretch your body.
This is a great way to warm up
your muscles.

Stretch like a cat,
this way and that!

Go!

Then you could go for a run.
Just run for fun!
Play tag with your friends.

Jog up a hill.
Then run down.
Jog back,
and jog to town.

Be on a Team

You can find out how to pitch and catch.
You can kick, toss, and pass a ball!

Be a Good Sport

Good sports try.

Good sports play fair.

Good sports have fun when they win and when they do not.

Do you know why it is fun to try?

It Is Up to You!

How will you get exercise?
Just get up and go!

If You Like to . . .   **You Can Try . . .**

run

jump

kick

118

READ Together

 Turn and Talk

Use details from **Get Up and Go!** to answer these questions with a partner.

1. Synthesize What is exercise? Why is exercise important for you?

2. What kinds of exercise can you do on your own? What kinds can you do with others?

Listening Tip

Listen carefully. Think of questions you want to ask your partner when it is your turn to talk.

Write an Opinion

PROMPT Which way of exercising from **Get Up and Go!** do you think is the best? Use details from the text to help you explain why.

PLAN First, write the kind of exercise you think is best. Write notes about your reasons why.

Reason	Reason	Reason

The best exercise is _____.

WRITE Now write sentences to tell which way of exercising you think is best. Tell reasons why. Remember to:

- Tell your opinion.

- Use the word **because** when you write a reason.

_____

- -

_____

- -

_____

- -

_____

- -

_____

- -

_____

- -

_____

Prepare to Read

GENRE STUDY **Fantasy** stories have made-up events that could not really happen. Look for:

- animals that talk and act like people

- a problem and resolution

- ways pictures and words help you understand

SET A PURPOSE Read to understand events in the beginning, middle, and end. Look for details in the words and pictures to help you. **Retell** the events in your own words.

POWER WORDS

graceful

talent

idea

Meet James Howe.

Brontorina

by James Howe

illustrated by Randy Cecil

Brontorina had a dream.

I want to dance!

"But you are a dinosaur," Madame Lucille
pointed out.

"True," Brontorina replied. "But in my heart,
I am a ballerina."

126

Madame Lucille wondered what to do. She had never had a dinosaur as a student before. Dinosaurs were rather large. And this one certainly did not have the right shoes.

But then she felt Clara and Jack tugging at her skirt. "Oh, please!" they pleaded.

Madame Lucille looked into the dinosaur's eyes. "What is your name, my dear?"

"Brontorina. Brontorina Apatosaurus. I even sound like a dancer, don't you agree?"

Madame Lucille did agree. How could she not?

"Welcome to Madame Lucille's Dance Academy for Girls and Boys," she said. "Please try not to squash the other dancers."

"Music, Magnolia!" she commanded the piano player.

Then Madame Lucille turned her commands to her students.

"What a graceful dancer you are, my dear!"
Madame Lucille exclaimed.

Brontorina blushed. "On the outside, I am
a dinosaur. But in my heart–"

"You are a ballerina!" cried Clara and Jack.

She still doesn't have the right shoes!

In the weeks that followed . . .

"Oh, Brontorina!" cried Madame Lucille. "I'm afraid you are too big to be a ballerina. You barely fit in my studio. And how in the world will a male dancer ever lift you over his head?"

A tear fell from Brontorina's eye.
Downcast, she turned to leave.

"Wait, Brontorina!" Clara called out. "Don't go. My mother has been working on a surprise for you. She is bringing it today."

"Whatever are you talking about?" Madame Lucille asked Clara.

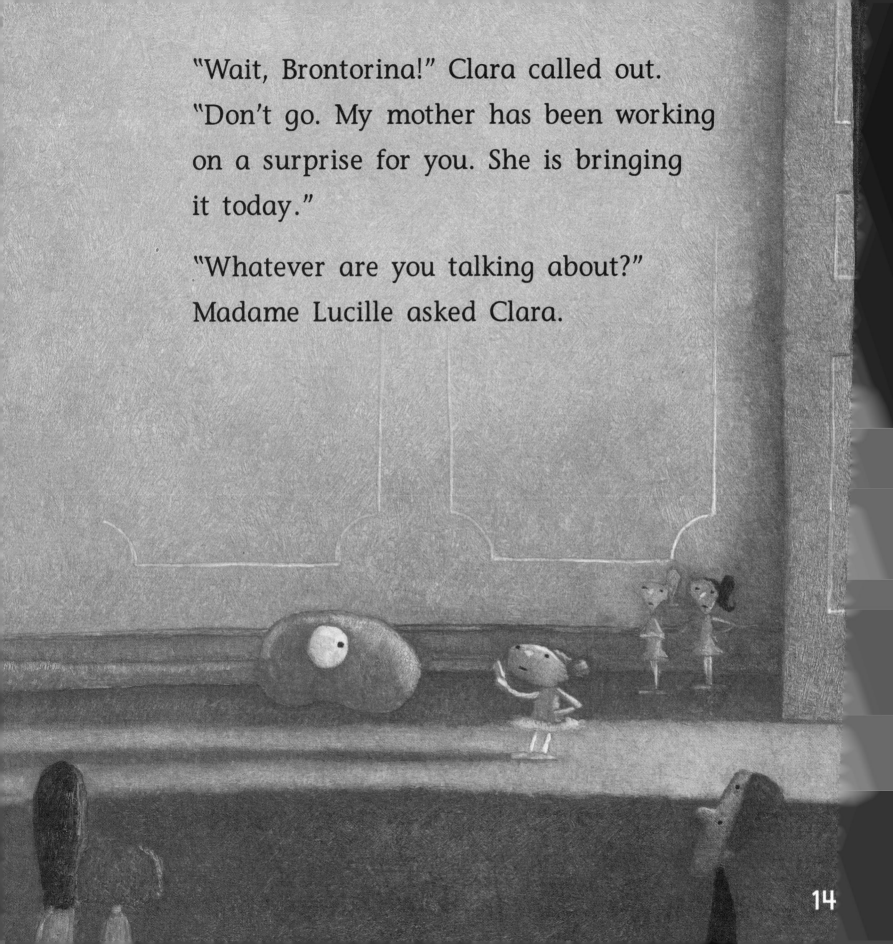

Just then, Clara's mother appeared at the door.

"You must be Brontorina," she said, holding out the surprise. "I hope these will fit."

Brontorina beamed. "They fit perfectly!" she cried. "I *am* a ballerina! Or I would be . . . if only I weren't so . . . big."

"Oh, fiddlesticks!" said Madame Lucille. "Why didn't I see it before? The problem is not that you are too big. The problem is that my studio is too small."

And so the whole class went off to
look for a studio big enough to hold
all of Brontorina's talent.

148

Still too small?

Still too small.

I have an idea!

149

Now Madame Lucille's dance academy had room for everyone.

MADAME LUCILLE'S

OUTDOOR DANCE ACADEMY

- FOR -

GIRLS AND BOYS AND DINOSAURS

AND COWS

I want to dance!

Then you must, my dear.

151

And it all began with a dream.

READ
Together

Turn and Talk

Use details from **Brontorina** to answer these questions with a partner.

1. **Retell** Tell the story in your own words. Tell about the main events that happen in the beginning, middle, and end.

2. How do Madame Lucille's ideas about Brontorina change during the story?

Talking Tip

Speak clearly. Do not speak too fast or too slow.

My idea is _____.

Write a Description

PROMPT How would you describe Brontorina to a new student at the dance school? Write a paragraph to explain. Use the story's pictures and words for ideas.

PLAN First, write words that describe Brontorina. Think about what she looks like and how she acts.

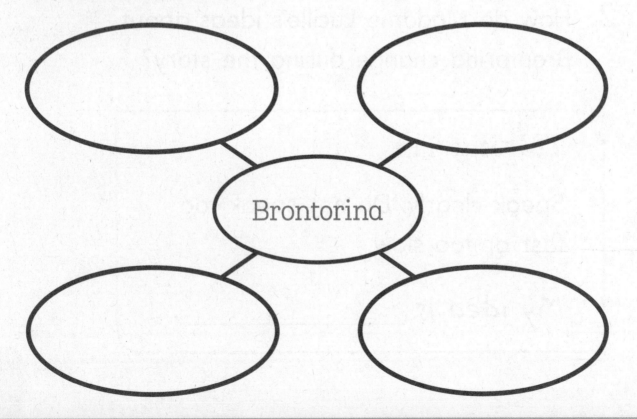

Brontorina

WRITE Now write to tell what Brontorina is like. Remember to:

- Find examples from the story.

- Use describing words to tell what she looks like and how she acts.

_____

- -

_____

_____

_____

- -

_____

_____

- -

_____

_____

- -

_____

Prepare to Read

GENRE STUDY ▶ **Fantasy** stories have made-up events that could not really happen. Look for:

• animals that act like people

• a lesson the characters learn

• ways pictures help you understand

SET A PURPOSE ▶ As you read, **make connections** to other things. Compare and contrast the text with other texts you have read. Think about how the text is like things in your life.

POWER WORDS

seed

short

heap

trouble

fruits

If You Plant a Seed

by Kadir Nelson

If you plant a tomato seed,

a carrot seed,

and a cabbage seed,

in time,

with love and care,

159

tomato,
    carrot,
        and cabbage
            plants will grow.

If you plant a seed
of selfishness,

in a very short time,

it will grow,

and grow,

166

and grow

167

into a heap

of trouble.

But if you plant

a seed of kindness,

169

in almost no time at all,

the fruits of kindness

will

grow,

and

grow,

and

grow,

172

173

and they are very, very sweet.

Turn and Talk

Use details from **If You Plant a Seed** to answer these questions with a partner.

1. **Make Connections** Think about what happens to all the friends in this story. How is this like what happens to the characters in **Brontorina**?

2. What do the characters do to be kind?

Listening Tip

Listen carefully. Look at your partner to show that you are paying attention.

Write a Book Report

PROMPT What lesson did you learn from **If You Plant a Seed**? Write a book report to tell others about the story and how you feel about it.

PLAN First, write about the lesson you learned. Write what you like and do not like about the story.

Lesson	I Like	I Do Not Like

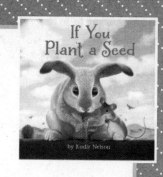

WRITE Now write your book report. First, tell the title. Tell about the lesson you learned. Then tell what you like or do not like. Use another sheet of paper if you need it. Remember to:

- Use the story for ideas.

- Give reasons for your opinions.

Prepare to View

GENRE STUDY **Videos** are short movies. Some videos give information. Others are for you to watch for enjoyment. Watch and listen for:

- how pictures and sounds work together
- how the video makes you feel
- a lesson you can learn

SET A PURPOSE Watch the video to find out what **topic** and **central idea** it shares. Look for details that help you understand it.

Build Background: Kindness

178

COLOR

Your World with Kindness

from BetterWorldians Foundation

As You View Notice when the pictures change from gray to color. What happens each time one person helps another? Use details like these to figure out what the main message of the video is.

Turn and Talk

COLOR
Your World with Kindness
from BetterWorldians Foundation

Use details from **Color Your World with Kindness** to answer these questions with a partner.

1. **Topic and Central Idea** What did you learn about the topic of kindness? Use details from the video to explain.

2. Describe the ways the people in the video help each other.

Talking Tip

Add on to what your partner says.

I think ____ because ____.

Let's Wrap Up!

(?) Essential Question

Why is it important to do my best and get along with others?

....

Pick one of these activities to show what you have learned about the topic.

1. Character Remix

Pick two characters from two different texts you read. Imagine that they meet. Draw a picture of them working together or being kind to each other. Write about your picture.

2. Dear Good Citizen

Write a letter to the character you read about who you think is the best citizen. Give reasons why he or she is the best. Read your letter to a partner. Talk about it.

Word Challenge

Can you use the word courtesy to help explain one of your reasons?

My Notes

Glossary

B

body   Your body is made up of all your parts, like your head, arms, and legs. You move your whole **body** when you dance.

C

camouflage   Camouflage is what hides something or makes it difficult to see. The animal's tan fur and spots are its **camouflage** in the grass.

characteristics   Characteristics are things that make a person, animal, or thing different from others. Short tails and long ears are **characteristics** of rabbits.

circling   If you are circling something, you keep moving around it in a circle. A bird was **circling** its nest before it landed in it.

coach   If you coach people, you tell and show them how to do something. My dad likes to **coach** my soccer team.

courtesy   If you do something as a courtesy, you do it to be kind or polite. He had the **courtesy** to help his grandma when it was raining.

D

dull When something is dull, it is not bright. It was a cloudy, **dull** day.

E

empty If something is empty, it does not have anything in it. I ate all my food, and now my bowl is **empty**.

equipment Your equipment is the stuff you need to play a game or do a job. We need helmets and other **equipment** to play football.

exclaimed If someone exclaimed something, it was said in an excited way. "Hooray!" the team **exclaimed** when they won.

exercise When you exercise, you move your body to get strong and healthy. We **exercise** when we ride our bikes.

F

fan If you are a fan of something, you like it very much. I cheer for the team since I am a big **fan**.

fruits The fruits of something are the good things that come from it. The **fruits** of trying hard are learning new things and feeling proud.

G

goal When you get a goal in a game, you get one or more points. I scored one **goal** in the game.

graceful If you are graceful, you move in a smooth and beautiful way. The **graceful** skater won the gold medal.

H

heap A heap is a lot of something. I have a **heap** of work to do today.

herd When you herd animals, you make them move together into a group. They **herd** the sheep into the barn.

honest If you are an honest person, you tell the truth. She was **honest** and told her mom she broke the cup.

I

idea An idea is a plan for how to do something. I have an **idea** for how to build a tree house.

M

mammal A mammal is a kind of animal that has hair and feeds milk to its babies. A whale is a **mammal**, and so are cats and people.

O

once   If you do something once another thing happens, you do it right after. I will do my homework **once** I finish eating.

P

predators   Predators are animals that hunt other animals for food. Little fish swim away from **predators** that want to eat them.

prey   An animal that is hunted by other animals is the prey. Fish are a bear's **prey**.

R

rules   Rules tell what you can and cannot do. We follow the **rules** when we play tag.

S

school   A big group of fish that swims together is called a school. A big **school** of fish swam by our boat.

seed   A seed is a small, hard part of a plant that grows into a new plant. A flower grew from the **seed** I planted in the dirt.

shingle   A shingle is a small, flat piece of wood, or something else, used to cover a roof. A big wind blew a **shingle** off our roof.

short   A short time is a small amount of time. We only waited a **short** time for the bus to come.

187

shriek   A shriek is a short, loud sound. I made a loud **shriek** when I saw a snake.

soon   If something will happen soon, it will happen a short time from now. School is over, so we will be home **soon**.

sport   A good sport plays fair and gets along with others. He is a good **sport** and has fun even if he loses.

stroll   When you take a stroll, you go on a slow walk. We took a **stroll** through the park.

surprise   A surprise is something you did not know you would see or do. The pet that Mom and Dad gave us was a big **surprise**!

T

talent   If you have a talent, you are naturally good at something. His wonderful singing **talent** made him a star.

team   A team is a group of people who play a game against another group. Our **team** won the game today!

thank   You thank people when they do something nice for you. I will **thank** him for the gift he gave me.

trouble   Trouble is a problem or something that is hard to fix. We had **trouble** finding our lost dog.

twigs   Twigs are small, thin branches from a tree or bush. The bird will build its nest with **twigs** from the tree.

W

warm   If something is warm, it is a little bit hot. I feel **warm** when I wear my hat and coat.

well   If you are well, you are healthy. I feel **well** after I go for a long walk.

Index of Titles and Authors

Acknowledgments

Brontorina by James Howe, illustrated by Randy Cecil. Text copyright © 2010 by James Howe. Illustrations copyright © 2010 by Randy Cecil. Reprinted by permission of Candlewick Press.

Have You Heard the Nesting Bird? by Rita Gray, illustrated by Kenard Pak. Text copyright © 2014 by Rita Gray. Illustration copyright © 2014 by Kenard Pak. Reprinted by permission of Houghton Mifflin Harcourt Publishing Company.

"How to Defend Yourself Like an Armadillo," "How to Spin a Web Like a Spider," and "How to Trap Fish Like a Humpback Whale" from *How to Swallow a Pig* by Steve Jenkins and Robin Page. Copyright © 2015 by Houghton Mifflin Harcourt. Reprinted by permission of Houghton Mifflin Harcourt Publishing Company.

If You Plant a Seed by Kadir Nelson. Copyright © 2015 by Kadir Nelson. Reprinted by permission of HarperCollins Publishers.

Credits

Blind iv *Animal* Q & A: (tl) ©flammulated/iStock/Getty Images Plus/Getty Images, (tr) ©Karel Gallas/Shutterstock, (bl) ©Guenter Fischer/Getty Images, (br) ©Flickr/Ewen Charl-ton/Getty Images; Blind vi *Good Sports:* (bg) ©Willard/iStock/Getty Images Plus/Getty Images, (c) ©FatCamera/iStock/Getty Images Plus/Getty Images; 2–3 (bg) ©Sharon Haeger/Shutterstock; 2–3 (bird's head poking out from nest) ©StanislavBelo-glazov/Shutterstock; 6 (standing penguin) ©flammulated/iStock/Getty Images Plus/Getty Images; 6 (penguin underwater) ©MikeCardUK/iStock/Getty Images Plus/Getty Images; 6 (tortoise) ©Karel Gallas/Shutterstock; 6 (Eastern box turtle on ground) ©Sean Wan-dzilak/Shutterstock; 7 (l) ©Guenter Fischer/Getty Images; 7 (elephant in water) ©Rems-berg Inc./Design Pics/Getty Images; 7 (r) ©Flickr/Ewen Charlton/Getty Images; 7 (hang-ing bat) ©cowboy5437/iStock/Getty Images Plus/Getty Images; 8 ©Jim Ruther Nill; 28 ©James Bruchac; 42 Courtesy of Houghton Mifflin Harcourt; 64 Courtesy of Houghton Mifflin Harcourt; 78 (inset) ©Chase Dekker Wild-Life Images/Getty Images; 78 (bg) ©UbjsP/Shutterstock; 79 (inset) ©All For You/Shutterstock; 80 ©National Geographic Stock; 82 ©Bertrand Demee/Photographer's Choice/Getty Images; 83 ©Holly Ku-chera/Shutterstock; 84 (c) (br) ©Patricia Doyle/Photographer's Choice/Getty Images; 84 (cl) ©Be Good/Shutterstock; 84 (r) ©MidoSemsem/Shutterstock; 84 (cr) ©Lane Oat-ey/Blue Jean Images/Getty Images; 84 (l) ©ImagesBazaar/Getty Images; 84 (c) ©Dmy-tro Zinkevych/Shutterstock; 84 (bg) ©Bimbim/Shutterstock; 88 (bg) ©Willard/iStock/Getty Images Plus/Getty Images; 88 (inset) ©FatCamera/iStock/Getty Images Plus/Getty Im-ages; 89 (tl) ©GagliardiImages/Shutterstock; 89 (tr) ©Blend Images/Alamy Images; 89 (br) ©Houghton Mifflin Harcourt; 90 ©Jane Medina; 92 ©AP/Houghton Mifflin Harcourt; 104 ©AP/Houghton Mifflin Harcourt; 108 ©Cristian Mallery Williams; 109 ©Blackout Con-cepts/Alamy; 110 ©FatCamera/iStock/Getty Images Plus; 110 (inset) ©Ivan Niku-lin/Shutterstock; 111 ©Sonya Etchison/Shutterstock; 111 (inset) ©Ivan Niku-lin/Shutterstock; 112 ©Monkey Business Images/iStock/Getty Images Plus; 112 (inset) ©Ivan Nikulin/Shutterstock; 113 ©Monkey Business Images/Getty Images; 113 (inset) ©Ivan Nikulin/Shutterstock; 114 ©Getty Images; 114 (inset) ©Ivan Nikulin/Shutterstock; 115 ©DenKuvaiev/iStockPhoto.com; 115 (inset) ©Ivan Nikulin/Shutterstock; 116 ©Getty Images; 116 (inset) ©Ivan Nikulin/Shutterstock; 117 ©FatCamera/iStock/Getty Images Plus; 117 (inset) ©Ivan Nikulin/Shutterstock; 118 (tc) ©Jim Erickson/Media Bakery; 118 (tl) ©Don Mason/Getty Images; 118 (tr) ©SHOTFILE/Alamy Images; 118 (bl) ©Double-PHOTO studio/Shutterstock; 118 (bc) ©warrengoldswain/iStock/Getty Images Plus; 118 (br) ©fakezzz/iStock/Getty Images Plus; 118 (cr) ©Blend Images/Alamy; 118 (c) ©JHershPhotography/iStock/Getty Images; 118 (cl) ©bradleym/iStock/Getty Images Plus; 118 (inset) ©Ivan Nikulin/Shutterstock; 118 (inset) ©Ivan Nikulin/Shutterstock; 118 (inset) ©Ivan Nikulin/Shutterstock; 178 ©Weekend Images Inc./Getty Images; 179 ©Bet-ter Worldians Foundation; 180 ©Better Worldians Foundation; 182 ©FatCam-era/iStock/Getty Images Plus; 183 ©Dragon Images/Shutterstock